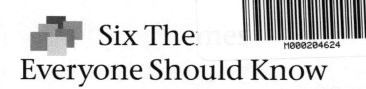

Six Themes Everyone Should Know

Jeremiah

W. Eugene March

Geneva
Press

First edition
Published by Geneva Press
Louisville, Kentucky

19 20 21 22 23 24 25 26 27 28—10 9 8 7 6 5 4 3 2 1

Cover designer: Rebecca Kueber

Library of Congress Cataloging-in-Publication Data

Names: March, W. Eugene (Wallace Eugene), 1935- author.
Title: Six themes in Jeremiah everyone should know / W. Eugene March.
Description: First edition. | Louisville, Kentucky: Geneva Press, 2019. |
   Series: Six themes everyone should know series
Identifiers: LCCN 2019001548 (print) | LCCN 2019016978 (ebook) | ISBN
   9781611649529 (ebk.) | ISBN 9781571532428 (pbk.: alk. paper)
Subjects: LCSH: Bible. Jeremiah--Theology.
Classification: LCC BS1525.52 (ebook) | LCC BS1525.52 .M36 2019 (print) |
   DDC 224/.206--dc23
LC record available at https://lccn.loc.gov/2019001548

Most Geneva Press books are available at special quantity discounts when purchased in bulk by corporations, organizations, and special-interest groups. For more information, please e-mail SpecialSales@GenevaPress.com.

Contents

Six Themes Everyone Should Know series

The Bible, by Barry Ensign-George

Genesis, by W. Eugene March

Matthew, by James E. Davison

Luke, by John T. Carroll

1 and 2 Timothy, by Thomas G. Long

Jeremiah, by W. Eugene March

Exodus, by V. Steven Parrish

Introduction to the
Six Themes Everyone Should Know series

The *Six Themes Everyone Should Know* series focuses on the study of Scripture. Bible study is vital to the lives of churches. Churches need ways of studying Scripture that can fit a variety of contexts and group needs. *Six Themes Everyone Should Know* studies offer a central feature of church adult educational programs. Their flexibility and accessibility make it possible to have short-term studies that introduce biblical books and their main themes.

Six Themes Everyone Should Know consists of six chapters that introduce major biblical themes. At the core of each chapter is an introduction and three major sections. These sections relate to key dimensions of Bible study. These sections ask:

- What does this biblical theme mean?
- What is the meaning of this biblical theme for the life of faith?
- What does this biblical theme mean for the church at this point in history for action?

This format presents a compact and accessible way for people in various educational settings to gain knowledge about major themes in the biblical books; to experience the impact of what Scripture means for Christian devotion to God; and to consider ways Scripture can lead to new directions for the church in action.

Introduction to *Jeremiah*

The noun "jeremiad" refers to a long, mournful complaint or lamentation. A "Jeremiah" is a pessimistic person; "jeremiad" is the way these Jeremiahs carry on. The biblical Jeremiah was seen as a prophet of judgment and doom, hence the etymological association.

It is an awesome responsibility to speak for God. Jeremiah, a spokesman for God, came from a family of priests. His father was Hilkiah. His ministry lasted some forty years (627–587 BCE). These were grim times. The powerful Babylonian Empire made war on Judah because, according to Jeremiah, the people and even the priests had sinned against God and had broken the covenant. Jeremiah spent his days lambasting the Hebrews for their false worship and social injustice and denouncing the king for his selfishness, materialism, and injustices. When not calling on his people to quit their wicked ways, he was lamenting his own lot; a portion of the Old Testament's book of Jeremiah is devoted to his "confessions," a series of lamentations on the hardships endured by a prophet with an unpopular message.

Jeremiah advised surrender in order to save lives and the city of Jerusalem. For this, he was branded a traitor. However, Jeremiah did not only pronounce judgment; he was also a prophet of hope, joy, and salvation for those who believed that God had not forsaken them, even when they went into exile. Jeremiah proclaims that the relationship with God, broken time and again, will be restored. Hope was not a luxury to be enjoyed by a few; it was strength for their survival.

During our own time of turmoil, may the study of Jeremiah bring you comfort and resolve to turn from the despair that crushes the human spirit and turn to the God of the covenant.

Biblical Backgrounds to Jeremiah

Author and Date

"First and foremost Jeremiah was a prophetic preacher rather than a writer, and the preservation of his messages in written form represents a secondary stage in their history. The prophet's use of Baruch the son of Neriah as a scribe to set down his messages in writing (36:4) strongly suggests that Baruch may have possessed special qualifications as a scribe-secretary."

"It is not the prophet himself, nor even his close associate Baruch, however, who has been responsible for the shaping of the present book. This has taken place in a circle of interpreters and scribes whose thinking and aims were closely, but not wholly, related to those of the Deuteronomistic school. . . . a body of thoughtful and intensely loyal Israelites who strove energetically to promote the true worship of Yahweh and to eradicate traces of the old Canaanite Baal religion in the period between 650 and 550 B.C."

—R. E. Clements, *Jeremiah*. Interpretation: A Bible Commentary for Teaching and Preaching (Louisville, KY: Westminster John Knox Press, 1988), 7, 12.

Major Concerns

"[Jeremiah]'s book is commentary upon the most disastrous episodes of Judah's history to which the Old Testament bears witness, both in their religious and political consequences."

"At one stroke the year 587 witnessed the removal of the two institutions—the temple and the Davidic kingship—which had stood as symbolic assurances of God's election of Israel. . . . What had happened demanded a total reappraisal and rethinking of Israel's self-understanding as the People of God."

—Clements, *Jeremiah*, 3, 6.

Importance

"Although many of the prophecies necessarily look back upon events belonging to an irreversible past, they did so in a manner designed to promote a deep and certain hope in the future and in the eventual restoration of Israel."

—Clements, *Jeremiah*, 3.

Jeremiah demonstrates what it can mean to be
embraced by God and claimed for special service.

Chapter 1

Jeremiah: A Prophet like Moses

Scripture
Jeremiah 1:4–19   God commissions Jeremiah.

Deuteronomy 18:15–22   A prophet like Moses will come.

Prayer
O awesome God, you have sought us across the centuries, inviting us into relationship with you. You have come to us in the person of prophets, in mighty acts of deliverance, and, finally, in the person of your Son Jesus, our Lord. Still we are often uncertain of your will. Help us now as we study the book of your prophet Jeremiah to gain the insight and perspective we need to live in the way you desire and relish. For Jesus' sake, hear our prayer. Amen.

Introduction
The book of Jeremiah is long, fifty-two chapters long. Jeremiah the prophet was active between the years 609 BCE and 585 BCE, witnessing and interpreting the fall of Judah to the Babylonians, including the exile of large numbers of Judean leaders to Babylon.

While the words and actions of the prophet Jeremiah are the focus of this long book, some other materials have been included because they agree with the theological perspective of Jeremiah or reflect on issues connected with him. The complex literary history of the book of Jeremiah will not be discussed in detail. Only let it be understood that the book was composed over at least a century and demonstrates theological reflection in its development.

Further, the book of Jeremiah is closely related in theology and literary style to parts of the book of Deuteronomy. Both Jeremiah and Deuteronomy insist that the proper foundation for Israel's relationship with God is the Mosaic covenant. After David had become king, a "royal ideology/theology" developed. Proponents of this perspective insisted that God's connection with Israel was mainly exercised through the Davidic monarch buttressed with a divine promise to David of an everlasting, unconditional covenant (2 Samuel 7; Psalm 89:1–38). Deuteronomy and Jeremiah challenged this understanding. They insisted that any relationship with God must be based on following the stipulations of the Ten Commandments and other parts of the covenant established by God with Moses and Israel at Sinai (Exodus 20:1–21; Deuteronomy 5:1–21), particularly the admonitions against idolatry.

The book of Jeremiah preserves the legacy of Jeremiah, son of Hilkiah, related to the priests of Anathoth, a village about three miles northeast of Jerusalem (Jeremiah 1:1). He was understood to be a "'prophet [*nabi'*] to the nations'" (1:5), a prophet like Moses (Deuteronomy 18:15). A *nabi'* was one commissioned by God to declare God's word. Such a prophet might say something about the future, but the main task was addressing the present. Biblical prophets *did not make predictions* about the future. They announced God's will for the present! That is how the book of Jeremiah is to be heard and understood.

A Basic Theme: Appointed over Nations and Kingdoms

The book of Jeremiah opens with the commissioning of the prophet (1:4–19). As Moses was given a word and task at the burning bush (Exodus 3:1–4:17), so Jeremiah received a word from God declaring him to be "'a prophet to the nations'" (1:5). As Moses resisted God's directive questioning whether he was capable of the assignment (Exodus 3:11), so Jeremiah responded with hesitancy, saying, "'I am only a boy'" (1:6). The Hebrew word translated "boy" is used of people of various ages, but seldom of children. It mainly suggests a level of experience. Here "young man" or "apprentice" might be a better translation since Jeremiah and his father were connected to the priestly circle at Anathoth. Whatever, it is highly unlikely that Jeremiah was a child.

The similarities between the accounts of Moses' and Jeremiah's commissioning continue. Both were assured that God would be with them no matter what they faced (Exodus 3:12; Jeremiah 1:8). And when Moses again tried to avoid the assigned task by citing his lack of speaking ability (Exodus 4:10–13), God reprimanded him and appointed Aaron to speak on Moses' behalf (Exodus 4:14–16). With Jeremiah, at the very beginning, God placed the divine word in his mouth (figuratively speaking, of course) and thereby assured Jeremiah that he was qualified to be a prophet (Jeremiah 1:14–15; see Deuteronomy 18:18).

Being a prophet was not something to covet. Often, Jeremiah faced a scornful, doubting king and people. Much of his task was to alert the nation, Judah, and its leaders, that God was deeply unhappy with them. They were in for a time of destroying, plucking up, and seeing reality as they had known it turned inside out (Jeremiah1:10). People never like to hear such words; the Judeans of Jeremiah's time were no different. As they rejected God, they also turned Jeremiah away, often violently. But Jeremiah was assured that God would be with him (1:8, 19).

The certainty of coming judgment was Jeremiah's fundamental message. This adverse consequence was the result of widespread idolatry (1:16). Because of this, Jeremiah has been seen as a negative person with no good news to share. While the judgments to come were frightening, there was nonetheless one good note to sound: a time "'to build and to plant'" was also part of God's word for Jeremiah to declare (1:10). God continued to have an interest in and a commitment to the people to whom Jeremiah was sent.

Yes, Jeremiah was a prophet like Moses. They were each commissioned with a word from God for a particular time. They were sent to confront royal power (Pharaoh in Egypt and a vassal puppet king in Judah). Nations and kingdoms stand under the lordship of God, no matter how powerful they may seem. And Moses and the prophet like Moses, Jeremiah, had a strong word to deliver.

The Life of Faith: Being Embraced by a Loving God

Reading about Jeremiah's induction into God's work is eye opening in several ways. First, from his own point of view, Jeremiah had nothing to qualify him for any significant role. Second, he was not particularly looking for a special task or opportunity of service. Third, as far as we are told, Jeremiah had no cause for which he had great zeal. He was more or less minding his own business when God burst in and distinctly claimed him.

Jeremiah was like many (most?) folk who today count themselves believers in God. In theory, God is important, but in personal terms God is absent. We do not know what Jeremiah was doing before God embraced him. Was he merely passing the time, hanging out, making do? Many seem to be doing that today. But after God claimed Jeremiah, things changed radically for him. He now had a purpose!

Few individuals are designated "prophets" by God. But God has an interest in each individual. God desires to embrace each one personally and assure each one of God's ongoing, caring presence. To reflect on Jeremiah's experience is to be reminded of God's intention and desire. Yes, there are times when God directs very particular messages through specific persons, like Moses or Jeremiah. But for the most part, God's purpose is advanced by ordinary folk, people who love God and who respond positively to God's prophets.

Those who recognize God's embrace are able to keep moving ahead even when circumstances are grim. They believe God's assurance of divine presence no matter what. Likewise, they recognize that divine displeasure is a real possibility that must be announced if social circumstances can be changed. So, as with Jeremiah, though not prophets themselves, they can and do take up the prophetic task of confronting others with God's word. This challenge belongs to all who care about God's desire for a peaceful and just world.

To understand and believe that one does not trudge through life alone and without any purpose changes one's outlook in significant ways. You don't ask that oft-repeated question "Is that all there is?" We do not live in isolation. We are part of a community with the God-given mission to live in the world in such a way that all may recognize the power and intent of God's embrace.

For a quarter of a century, Jeremiah carried out his assignment. He was generally ignored, though sometimes he was attacked. What sustained him throughout his service was the assurance of

God's presence. That same assurance continues to be extended to any and all who will trust in God's word. Many have claimed such a trust, but their way of life does not reflect such a commitment. Personal joy comes in accepting God's embrace and celebrating each step forward toward God's goal of a just peace for all people.

The Church: Living Out Jeremiah's Call

Jeremiah was "'appointed . . . a prophet to the nations'" (Jeremiah 1:5c). Today the church is challenged to continue this mission. To do this will require several different strategies, some directed at the church itself and others aimed at the wider society:

A fundamental realignment of the church's priorities needs to be made. The goal is not to expand the church (though that may at times occur). The goal is to engage the "nations." Jeremiah was given authority to reprimand nations and kingdoms. He was instructed to enter the realm of politics. For him, religion had a grave responsibility for society. The social and political structures that humans had created were the targets of Jeremiah's declarations. To the degree that these foster injustice and/or inequality they are to be removed.

The church continues to have such a commission. There is a problem, however, in that many church members claim that religion and politics should be kept separate. Religion, they argue, has only to do with the "spiritual" and nothing to do with economics, justice systems, military operations, and so forth. Such a position has hampered the church for centuries. It contradicts Jeremiah, most of the other prophets, and Jesus himself. The church must give significant attention to this misunderstanding if it is to continue Jeremiah's assignment.

Our society's economic structure that rewards acquisition is in dire need of attention. For many, to gain riches and authority is the whole aim of life. Only by accumulating an overabundance of "things" can security be achieved (it is claimed). Thus, any behavior is justified so long as the goal is personal or national wealth and security. This is sometimes the result of unregulated capitalism.

There is no easy solution to this problem. A good, workable way for the "haves" to share fairly with the "have-nots" has yet to be developed. The church needs to encourage research and practice toward finding solutions. But again, many in the church do not understand this to be the church's business. Education and a change in priorities are yet necessary.

The recognition that God is sovereign over all kingdoms and nations is often denied directly or indirectly. For some, only the United States, or perhaps Israel, can claim any special relationship with God. But that is not the message of Jeremiah or the other prophets. All nations and peoples belong to God. Many believe that divine judgment should fall on other nations. Jeremiah had a major job to do in convincing the people of Judah that they were just as responsible before God as the people of Assyria or Babylon. For many Christians in the United States, there is a similar denial of responsibility before God. Other nations, not the United States, deserve punishment. Jesus warned us to take care of the log in our own eye before worrying about the speck in the eye of another (Luke 6:41).

For Reflection and Action

1. How have you personally experienced a sense of God's absence? Of God's presence?

2. What difference does a sense of purpose add to a person's life?

3. What are some appropriate ways for the church to engage in political action? Are there inappropriate ways?

4. Read Jeremiah 1 several times, and then read Romans 13:1–10, and compare the texts. How is Jeremiah to be tempered by Romans? How is Romans 13:1–7 to be corrected by Jeremiah? What difference does Romans 13:8–10 make in the discussion?

God's anger springs from God's dismay and disappointment over the disobedience of the Judean king and people. God's dismay is not irrational.

Chapter 2

The Angry Dismay of God

Scripture

Jeremiah 2:1–3:5a   God indicts Judah for breach of covenant.

Jeremiah 48:1–47   God announces Moab's doom for Moab's disobedience.

Prayer

Gracious God, patient God, enable us to recognize and acknowledge when our behavior brings dismay and anger to you. Help us to turn from such action and make a more determined effort to do your will. We desire to please you and honor you. Guide us and strengthen us in our efforts. Hear our prayer for Jesus' sake. Amen.

Introduction

Two sections of Jeremiah are sampled in this chapter. First, Jeremiah 2:1–3:5a is part of a large group of oracles found in Jeremiah 2–25. An oracle is a message communicated in some manner by God that the prophet fashions into a word for the people. This part of Jeremiah repeatedly announces God's extreme displeasure with Judah's king and people during the years from 605 BCE to 587 BCE. As a result, the destruction of Judah and the exile of many are announced.

The second group of texts to be considered constitutes what are called the "Oracles against the Nations" (Jeremiah 46–51).

This material has parallels in Isaiah 13–23 and Ezekiel 25–32. This material may have been circulated separately before being placed in the present context in Jeremiah. The dating of these chapters is problematic, but they do contain references to events after the death of Jeremiah.

Throughout each of these groups of texts (2–25; 46–51), a picture of God emerges that many people find disturbing. God reacts to the conduct of those addressed in Judah (and other nations as well) with deep disappointment to the point of anger. God's reaction is not merely the outrage of a toddler denied some toy. No, God's response is triggered by behavior that God considers wrong, entirely in defiance of commandments intended to promote justice and allegiance to the Lord God. God's is a morally prompted anger.

This picture of God, however, disturbs a widely assumed notion that God should always be sweet and happy like a doting grandparent with grandchildren. God is thought by some always to be even-tempered, even indulgent, with people when they make "mistakes." Jeremiah's oracles of judgment, however, show God's dismay and disgruntlement at the behavior of the Judean king and people and of leaders of other nations as well. But to assume that the God of the Old Testament is simply a "god of wrath" and to dismiss these texts as "unworthy" of God is to ignore God's complexity. Misunderstanding of both the Old and New Testaments is a possible result.

A Basic Theme: The Reality of Divine Dismay

God is deeply troubled by the people of Judah. God remembered when they were utterly devoted, following God in the wilderness and being protected as "holy to the LORD" (2:2–3). That was how it was supposed to be. That was then, but now is now.

Jeremiah's word from the Lord describes a different situation. For some reason that God did not understand, the people went after "worthless things and became worthless themselves" (2:5). God brought the people out of Egypt through the wilderness into a fruitful land (2:6–7a). But once there, the people and their leaders went after other deities. In so doing they violated the covenant oaths they had taken at Sinai (2:7b–8; cf. Exodus 24:1–8; Deuteronomy 10:12–22). This is beyond God's comprehension. How could God's people have exchanged their gods, their glory, for something worthless (2:11)? Through Jeremiah the depth of God's dismay is expressed:

> Be appalled, O heavens, at this,
>> be shocked, be utterly desolate,
>>> says the LORD,
>> for my people have committed two evils:
>> they have forsaken me,
>> the fountain of living water,
>>> and dug out cisterns for themselves,
>> cracked cisterns
>>> that can hold no water. (2:12–13)

Jeremiah is unrelenting in detailing the ways the people have violated their relationship with God. The "fear" [awesome respect] of God was gone (2:19). They pursued the Baals (Canaanite fertility deities; 2:23); trees and rocks were worshiped as divine (2:27). The "lifeblood of the innocent poor" is found on their skirts (2:34). In their disobedience, the people and the king "have played the whore with many lovers [false deities]" (3:1). In the chapters that follow, these and other charges are leveled against the Judeans! God was, and had a right to be, dismayed and, yes, angry.

In the oracle against Moab, similar dismay is expressed. The Moabites are not charged with breaking a covenant with God. However, in the book of Amos, Moab is charged with defiling the bones of a defeated king, which was considered a breach in international "law." Possibly something like the Geneva Conventions forbade such behavior (Amos 2:1). Such breaches in conduct may be behind some of the hostility felt by other people against the Moabites (Jeremiah 48:1–6). Moab trusted in its own power and "magnified himself against the LORD" (48:42). For their pride and insolence the Moabites were to be destroyed (48:29–30). This was not the result of a "divine temper tantrum" or of something the Moabites had done against Israel. No, Moab "earned" what it was to receive.

The oracles we have briefly reviewed are undoubtedly negative in tone and do not present a pleasant picture for Judah or Moab. But these oracles are not irrational outbursts by a wrathful deity.

They reflect divine dismay at the actions of the people, dismay that has led to God's anger. Nonetheless, even still, a word of hope is extended to Judah and Israel (3:12–14) and to hapless Moab as well (48:47).

The Life of Faith: Acknowledging the Reality of Divine Anger

One of the most challenging faith issues to deal with is the matter of God's anger. If God is love, how can there be anger? This seems a reasonable question; an answer is suggested by merely reviewing the behavior of parents, teachers, spouses, siblings, and friends. All of us experience anger at times with those we may love the most. The occurrence of anger and love in the same person even at the same time is not really the issue.

The problem for many is that we have been taught that anger is bad, wrong, and certainly "ungodly." First, then, we have to get beyond the idea that anger is sinful. Some anger may be, but not all anger by any means. It is not wrong to be angry at injustice, abuse, bullying, and the like. There are many situations where anger is healthy and helpful. To the degree that this presents a psychological problem, then work on that.

In Jeremiah's context, however, there is another issue. Can God really have "emotions"? Greek philosophy said, "No; absolutely not." By definition God was "impassable," the philosophers argued. God was incapable of having any feelings at all; impossible to engage emotion, unable to suffer. Part of that understanding prohibits thinking that God can get angry. But if that is so, then God cannot know love either. The Bible, of course, does not speak of God as "impassable." Quite the contrary! So much of that which has come to us by way of Greek philosophy and classical medieval theology needs to be jettisoned.

Another difficulty rests with the gospel message that by Jesus' death and resurrection we have been judged and forgiven. That is undeniably true! But that does not mean that God cannot be pained by or get angry at human behavior. God's capacity to have and express what we call "emotions" is beautifully described in Exodus (34:6–7) and in a number of other texts (Numbers 14:18; Nehemiah 9:17; Psalms 86:15; 103:8; 145:8; Jeremiah 32:18; Joel 2:13; Jonah 4:2; Nahum 4:1–3). God can forgive and still get angry—just like we can! God can love and yet be disappointed.

God can even be uncertain of what is going on at times—that is probably the most surprising point our brief consideration of Jeremiah's oracles has uncovered.

So how are we to embody what we have learned about God through Jeremiah? The prophet may be our best guide. Jeremiah was instructed to buy a field right at the height of the Babylonian attack on Judah (32:6–8). Not a smart time to invest in real estate! How could God punish and deliver at the same time? Jeremiah did not know (32:25), but he acted anyway. The theological puzzle we have acknowledged cannot be solved entirely. Questions remain, but action cannot be postponed while we ponder this issue. In faith we make the best choices we can, trusting God's love to sustain us.

The Church: Announcing God's Displeasure

A primary task of the church today is declaring the grave displeasure God has with the manner in which people are treated, individually and as groups. The church is not going to be able to address and correct all of the injustices and iniquities that exist. Instead, the church must choose to "meddle" where it thinks the most can be done, using these efforts as signals to point to all that needs reform.

From Jeremiah, several issues may be highlighted. God is not pleased with the ill-treatment of individuals, particularly the poor, by the powerful. Too many have become "great and rich . . . fat and sleek" at the expense of orphans and the rights of the needy (5:27–28). There is ample evidence of this in our society. The jails are filled with people (mostly of color) who have committed only minor offenses while people with the means of hiring proper legal assistance go unpunished. There are "fast-loan" operations where the poor are charged incredible rates of interest to get a loan to tide them over for a brief time until their next paycheck arrives. Some people cannot arrange a mortgage because they do not have a proper credit record (for example, recently graduated students or divorced women who did not work outside the home while raising children). Some of these difficulties are the result of individual irresponsibility, but many are caused by bias and prejudice in the broader society.

A longer list of "wrongs"—things that Jeremiah contended displease God—could easily be constructed. For instance, nothing has been said of the corruption of religion and the abandonment of tradition occurring in our society. "False gods"—wealth, social status, educational achievement, political power, and so on—everywhere abound. These are the Baals of our time and are no less destructive of a genuine relationship with God than in the time of Jeremiah.

On some issues, political efforts need to be launched. New laws may be necessary to reform the situation. This apparently is not easy to accomplish and usually takes much time and effort. For many churches, it is a challenging task because of a false notion that religion should stay out of politics. Jeremiah certainly did not believe that to be true.

But on many other issues, personal and local effort can be applied to great benefit. Caring for the ill and aging, for instance, can enable help to reach the needy. At the same time, such action can help those rendering the assistance to gain a more healthy and helpful understanding of themselves and the broader situation. Or reaching out to the lonely—whether they are newly arrived folk, the homeless, or people without family—can deeply enrich all involved.

The inequities and difficulties that rend the fabric of our society are a concern for God as for us. When we do harm to one another by intention or neglect, we bring pain to God.

For Reflection and Action

1. Carefully read Luke 11:37–54. How does Jeremiah support Luke's presentation of Jesus? How can we be good citizens of our nation and maintain sole allegiance to God? Do Jesus' words in Luke 11:37–54 help or confuse the issue?

2. What are some of the ways to "explain" or "unpack" the difficulty of acknowledging that God can become angry?

3. Construct a list of problems in your community that Jeremiah might consider displeasing to God.

4. How might your class or congregation try to address a particular matter of injustice or need in your local area? Develop a plan of action.

Chapter 3

The Mosaic Way Is
God's Desired Way

Scripture
Jeremiah 7:1–15   Jeremiah delivers a Temple sermon.

Jeremiah 26:1–24   Reaction to Jeremiah's message.

Prayer
O God of the prophets, continue to guide us. We are grateful for
the prophets you have sent. We know we are stubborn and inat-
tentive. Enable us to hear them and to follow your instruction.
Provide us with the eyes to see and the ears to hear your word. In
Jesus' name we pray. Amen.

Introduction
The book of Jeremiah has a significant amount of poetic material
that has been partially explored in previous chapters. There is also
a great deal of prose, both biographical and autobiographical. The
prose sections provide much information about the historical
situation in which Jeremiah worked and about the prophet as a
person.

The biographical material is concentrated in chapters 26–45.
Baruch, Jeremiah's disciple and scribe (see 32:12–16; 36:10, 32;
43:3, 6; 45:1–5), is thought by some scholars to have been the
writer/editor of this material. A number of prose sermons are found
(7:3–8:3; 11:3–14; 16:1–13; 17:19–27; 18:1–12; 21:1–10; 25:1–24)

15

in the largely poetic section of the book (1–25). Within these are some details that might be autobiographical (from Jeremiah himself) which supplement the biographical material.

Most of the work of Jeremiah was done in the last twenty years or so of Judah's existence as a political state (609–585 BCE). The times were tumultuous. A lengthy period of Assyrian rule over the Middle East came to its end in 609 with the Babylonians taking over that role. Judah was a vassal first of Assyria (701–609 BCE), briefly Egypt (609–605 BCE), and then Babylon. Babylon brought an end to Judah. Three times Judean leaders were exiled to Babylonia (597, 587, 585 BCE). The rightful king was replaced with a "puppet" appointed by and loyal to Babylon.

Jeremiah was directed to address his king and the people of Judah at a time of great trouble (mainly between 609–585 BCE). War continued to ravage the nation. The economy was in bad shape. Religion was profoundly messed up. There was a great fear among the people and very little hope that things could be righted.

Jeremiah was given the extremely distressing task of declaring to the Judeans that God was extremely displeased with them! Why wasn't God angry at the invading Babylonians for their vicious attacks? Eventually, the acts of Babylon would be addressed (50:1–52:34), but during most of his years of work, Jeremiah had to remonstrate his own people. He had to live with some tough questions, some strong doubts about the justice of God.

A Basic Theme: God's Preference for the Mosaic Way

In 609 BCE, a crisis occurred in Judah that Jeremiah was told to address. Josiah, king of Judah, was killed in a battle at Megiddo with an Egyptian army led by Pharaoh Neco (2 Kings 24:28–29). Josiah had reigned since 639. In 620 a scroll was found during repair work being done on the Temple in Jerusalem. Huldah, the prophetess, verified it as authentic (2 Kings 22:14). It came to be called the book of the covenant. The content of the scroll prompted Josiah to conduct a thorough reform. The reform featured removing all the idols and other signs of idolatrous worship in Judah, particularly in the Temple (2 Kings 22:8, 16–17; 23:1–3, 4–23). Many scholars believe that scroll was an early version of the book of Deuteronomy.

When Josiah died in 609, what had been accomplished in the reform was put aside, and the people turned back to the idolatry they had practiced previously. Since it seemed that God had not protected Josiah, the reform was considered senseless. In 605 Jeremiah addressed the people at the Temple, lambasting them and their new king for turning back from the teaching of the book of the covenant. Jeremiah declared a disaster was about to fall on Judah with the destruction of the land and the Temple. This "sermon" is reported in Jeremiah 7 with a description of the outcome in Jeremiah 26.

A survey of Jeremiah's words makes it clear that he was sure the Mosaic covenant had been cast aside. The people were putting false trust in the Temple (7:4). They had decided to trust in the royal ideology that assured the people of God's protection of the Temple and the Davidic king (2 Samuel 7; Isaiah 29:1–8; Psalms 89; 132). They seemingly ignored the Ten Commandments conveyed via Moses (Exodus 20:1–17; Deuteronomy 5:6–21; Jeremiah 7:8–10). Idolatry was rampant (Jeremiah 7:30–31). Jeremiah explicitly noted that the people had ignored the covenantal promise (7:23–24). Despite God's repeated efforts to bring the people back, they resisted (7:25–26).

The reaction to Jeremiah's word was swift and negative. Many people immediately declared Jeremiah deserving of punishment because he announced the destruction of Jerusalem and the Temple (26:7–11). When Jeremiah would not back down, a debate broke out about whether Jeremiah deserved death. Citing the precedent of Micah of Moresheth (see Micah 3:9–12), who, though he had also announced the destruction of Zion, had been spared, Jeremiah's advocates prevailed. Jeremiah was not killed (26:16–19). Another prophet with the same message, however, was put to death (26:20–23).

Essential to Jeremiah's theology was the conviction that God had entered into a covenant with the people at Sinai. At that time Moses was the prophet who spoke God's word, and thus we have the Mosaic covenant. Jeremiah sought to call the people back to the observance of that covenant with its strong emphasis on personal behavior (for example, the Ten Commandments) and the rejection of every form of idolatry.

The Life of Faith: Seeking to Live in God's Way

It sounds somewhat old-fashioned to suggest living in a pattern offered to our forbearers centuries ago. Many would argue that modern times require up-to-date directions and norms. "Mosaic" sounds merely antiquated or utterly legalistic. But it is to this standard that Jeremiah calls us, a standard not unlike that of Jesus of Nazareth.

There are three essential motifs for living in God's way:

The Lord alone is worthy of worship. "I am the LORD your God, who brought you out of the land of Egypt, out of the house of slavery; you shall have no other gods before me" (Deuteronomy 5:6; see also Exodus 20:2; Matthew 22:37–38; Mark 12:29–30). Idolatry is absolutely forbidden! Now that seems clear-cut, and goodness knows, we do not go around setting up altars on every corner to make offerings to various deities. But actually, it isn't all that easy. A "god" is anything/anyone who claims our absolute allegiance. That can be a job, a summer resort, a spouse, children, a 401(k) account, a position of privilege on a board, a . . . well, *anything* that claims first place in our lives. When considered this way, the prohibition against idolatry perhaps sounds different and a good deal more pertinent. Such lesser— but nonetheless real—"gods" can influence our life choices in any manner of ways. They are tough to eliminate. Only with the help of others can this adequately be accomplished.

Personal behavior matters. The Ten Commandments begin with the admonition about having no other gods, but the other commandments are also crucial for a healthy community. It is common sense to be against stealing, murdering, committing adultery, and allowing false oaths (swearing falsely) in court. A community cannot survive for long if such behavior goes unchecked. It is the responsibility of each person to reject such action. Jesus set a high standard (see Matthew 5:21–48), but Jesus also loved all people, especially sinners who did not meet his mark.

The social fabric simply cannot survive unless those who act in such ways are held accountable. This has been done in a variety of ways. A legalistic approach of shunning or public humiliation has been used, but it is indeed not what Jesus would recommend (e.g., Luke 6:9–11; 7:36–50; John 8:11). Individual example and personal intervention are probably the best avenues to follow. Grace, not law, is the proper guide.

Our relationship with God is finally and entirely dependent upon God. This third motif is the most important. Jeremiah repeatedly assured his people of God's willingness to forgive (3:12–14, 22; 7:5–7, 23). This conviction was shared by many other prophets, especially Isaiah (e.g., Isaiah 43:1–7, 25–28; 51:4–8; 55:6–9). Our Lord Jesus is the ultimate assurance of God's love and intention to deliver us (Romans 8:1–4). We cannot earn or win God's forgiveness! That is a gracious gift.

The Church: A Time to Speak Out

Speaking out in God's name is critical at this time and much more difficult than it has sometimes been. Why? First of all, because a sizeable percentage of the people of our country don't really believe that there is a God; or, if there is, that God has any power to affect the world. Yes, the polls continue to say that a majority of people in the United States believe in God, but their behavior doesn't back that up. They do not regularly attend or participate in the work of a faith community. They often try to hedge the question by saying they are "spiritual," not "religious." They show little awareness of the biblical tradition or the actions that tradition encourages. They may believe in God. They are what might be called "holy-days Christians," showing up only on Christmas and Easter.

This is important, for many of the difficulties encountered in our society result, in the long run, from various forms of idolatry. We cannot easily use this language because our culture doesn't readily admit that there are any gods, let alone false gods. Yet from within the biblical tradition that is the problem. During this study, we have indicated a number of the usual non-gods (such as money, prestige, power) that are worshiped by many, many people, some without even knowing that that is what they are doing.

One of the most pernicious is false nationalism. It is not wrong or injurious to be proud of one's homeland. Citizens of the United

States, for instance, have much of which rightly to boast. We have come to the aid of numerous folk in grave difficulty around the world, either militarily or economically, and that is to be praised. Many immigrants have found refuge in this country. Women certainly have greater freedom here than in many other parts of the world.

But things are far from perfect. At present, a false nationalism is being promoted that claims God gives special privilege to the United States. It claims that anyone who criticizes the United States or its leaders is out to destroy the country. Some believe that "white" is the only color true Americans can be. Many of these claims are put forward as the teachings of the Bible and God's will. Jeremiah would not agree, nor would Jesus, nor should we.

False nationalism is a devious form of idolatry, and it needs to be so labeled. To resist it will not be easy or pleasant. Some will claim any criticism of the nation as an attack on Christianity. Nonetheless, false nationalism is as potentially destructive for us as Baalism was for the Judah of Jeremiah's time. False nationalism must be addressed from the pulpit, in church school, in the church press, and any other way possible. It is a false god the worship of which can prove fatal.

For Reflection and Action
1. Read Romans 13:1–10, and discuss how these verses expand/ restrict Jeremiah's understanding of his relationship to the government of his day. Add Mark 12:28–34 to the conversation. How are we to understand our relation to our nation?

2. What are some of the differences in what some call our national "values" and what Jeremiah understood as the Mosaic way?

3. Name some of the "false gods" that you see in our society. How do they affect our national life? Your personal life?

4. In what ways can the church aid, support, or correct those caught up in the conflict over national policies that challenge the right to disagree with the national government?

*Recognizing and accepting the reality of God's pain is
critical and difficult if people are to turn away from
the behavior that causes that pain.*

Chapter 4

Sharing God's
Frustration and Pain

Scripture
Jeremiah 12:1–13   Jeremiah complains to God.

Jeremiah 15:5–9, 15–18, 19–21   God indicates that punishment
is inevitable, but that punishment does not have to be the end.

Jeremiah 18:19–23   The people plot against Jeremiah.

Prayer
Merciful God, Jeremiah was acutely aware of the pain the disobedience of your people caused you. He shared your pain and your
suffering. Grant that we may catch a glimpse of what you experience and join with Jeremiah in sharing some of that discomfort.
Hear our prayer, for we offer it through Jesus our Lord. Amen.

Introduction
The material in this chapter belongs to a style, type, or genre of
literature often found in the Bible, particularly in the Psalms.
Across several centuries of scholarly work, the poems in this literary form came to be called "laments." In the course of time,
language changed. It is now recognized that this type of psalm
does not represent a "lament" in the modern American English
sense of that word. Rather, it presents a "supplication" or perhaps
a "complaint."

Psalms of supplication are numerous. Some are the expressions of individuals (for example, Psalms 3–7, 13, 22). Others express a community's concern (for example, Psalms 44, 60, 74, 79). These psalms voice very directly, often very bluntly, a difficulty (persecution by others, drought, defeat, illness) that the supplicant wants God to remedy or explain. "Why, O God . . ." is sounded frequently. Calls to "rescue us," "restore us," "heal us" are heard repeatedly. Since God is ultimately responsible for all of life, God is not allowed to go unchallenged.

Parts of many poems in Jeremiah have strong parallels to the psalms of supplication or complaint (for example, Jeremiah 12, 15, 16, 17, 18, 20). Strong language is used. The images are vivid. The accusations against God are specific and bold. What must be understood in this poetic tradition is that it was not considered wrong or impious to express honest feelings. When the prophet thought God was not being fair or just, the prophet said so! The good news for us is that God shot right back and wouldn't let the prophet or people off the hook either. God was not offended by honest expressions of uncertainty or disagreement. The psalm of supplication is a model for us of how to come clean before God with our doubts and pain. And what's more, in these exchanges between God and Jeremiah, we learn that God too had concerns, sorrows, and disappointments, resulting from the continued rebellion of his people.

A Basic Theme: The Prophet Shares God's Pain

It is very important to understand at the beginning that God is frustrated by and very much in pain over Judah's behavior. We sometimes forget this. At the very outset God is heard by the prophet saying:

> My anguish, my anguish! I writhe in pain! . . .
> "For my people are foolish,
>   they do not know me;
> they are stupid children,
>   they have no understanding.
> They are skilled in doing evil,
>   but do not know how to do good." (4:19a, 22)

God cares and is in pain over Judah's coming destruction!

It is this pain that Jeremiah knows and shares but does not understand. "Why does the way of the guilty prosper? Why do all who are treacherous thrive?" (12:1). Jeremiah, rather like Job (Job 31:1–40), wants to know why God allows this. God responds quite sharply: "If you have raced with foot-runners and they have wearied you, how will you compete with horses? And if in a safe land you fall down, how will you fare in the thickets of the Jordan?" (12:5). In other words, God reprimands Jeremiah for his complaint. Things are going to get a lot worse. His own family will turn against him (12:6). God's pain is more significant than Jeremiah has imagined, for as God says:

> I have forsaken my house,
>   I have abandoned my heritage;
> I have given the beloved of my heart
>   into the hands of her enemies.
> My heritage has become to me
>   like a lion in the forest;
> she has lifted up her voice against me—
>   therefore I hate her. (12:7–8)

Jeremiah has his own pain. God has told Jeremiah not to marry or have children (16:2). Jeremiah cursed the day he was born (20:14–18). Because of his oracles, the leaders plotted against Jeremiah (18:23, 20; 20:1–2, 10; 36:19, 26). Jeremiah wanted vindication, namely the destruction of his enemies (17:14–18; 18:21–23). These were not noble thoughts by Jeremiah, but they honestly reflected his feelings. God can handle that.

Jeremiah was also angry with God for giving him such an assignment. He accused God of having "enticed" (Hebrew, "seduced") him and "overpowered" him, forcing him to deliver God's painful message (20:7). As a result, Jeremiah had become a "laughingstock" (20:7). People mocked Jeremiah because his words seemed unfulfilled. God's word to Jeremiah had become a "reproach and derision" because judgment had not come to pass (20:8)! At times Jeremiah was so upset with God that he wanted to say nothing at all, but God's word was too much, and Jeremiah couldn't remain silent (20:9).

Through all of this Jeremiah nonetheless puts his confidence in God to surely bring vindication (17:9–11; 20:12). Jeremiah knows his pain and God's as well. He cannot understand "why," but he trusts God to protect him (15:20) and deliver him (15:21). That is all he can count on, and he does.

The Life of Faith: Recognizing and Responding to God's Pain

Before we can make a proper response to God's frustration and pain, we have to understand that God can, in fact, experience these feelings. They are quite familiar to human beings, but for centuries they have been denied as possible for God. There have been at least two regrettable consequences of this assumption:

The Old Testament has been wrongly claimed to represent God as wrathful, vengeful, and hateful. This represents a vast misunderstanding. Yes, God does bring judgment on those so deserving, but God does not do so gleefully. Jeremiah testifies to the frustration and pain God experiences in such situations.

It is very difficult to understand Jesus Christ if God is not recognized as participating in the suffering of Jesus. When Jesus prayed in the Garden of Gethsemane, he sought God's assurance (Luke 22:39–46). Using Psalm 22—a psalm of supplication!—to express his pain and despair (Matthew 27:46), Jesus cried out from the cross, "'My God, my God, why have you forsaken me?'" When he wept over Jerusalem, he demonstrated God's pain over a wayward people (Luke 19:41–44). Yes, Jeremiah and Jesus knew well the divine capacity for suffering and disappointment.

Remembering that, we too must claim our share of the pain known by God. In the first place, we continue to bring such pain to our God. The proper response is not to melt in sorrow and guilt. As appropriate as such feelings may be at times, it is better for us to cease the behavior that brings God disappointment. Instead of just feeling sorry, we need to turn away from such actions. Yes, they may well be "sinful," but that is not the most urgent problem. More importantly, our deceit, our disdain for others, our selfishness, these bring anguish to our God! Until we understand this, it is unlikely that we will be able seriously to repent or live the life God hopes for us.

Recognizing and sharing in God's pain can equip us, on the one hand, to better accept who we are, and, on the other hand, to care for one another. Getting angry is not evil in itself. Even God gets angry. But what we do with our anger is another question. We need to turn it outward, not inward. Self-depreciation will not move us to accept the love of God. Anger aimed at self is merely another form of self-indulgence, and it is that from which God seeks to free us. At the same time, admitting that we get angry can help us better relate to others. They too may lose their patience or their civility; that, unfortunately, is human. But if we can allow it without bashing it, we may have taken a step toward peace. Recognizing the reality of anger, disappointment, and pain are first steps toward living the kind of life, with the help of God's Spirit, that Paul urges for us (Galatians 5:19–23).

The Church: Sharing God's Dismay

For centuries the church has presented the God of the Old Testament as a God of judgment. Besides being, at best, only partially untrue, this caricature of the Old Testament has opened the door for anti-Jewish ideologies, which bring discredit to the church. The message of the Old Testament is that God created a good world and continues to care for it and all the people in it. So what might be done to correct this distorted view of the Bible?

There are at least two ways to address this problem:

There needs to be a concerted effort in the church to correct the misinformation. The God of the Old Testament is the Creator and the One incarnated in Jesus of Nazareth. There are not two "gods," one of the Old Testament—a wrathful deity—and a second of the New Testament—a gracious, forgiving deity. There is but one God, the Creator of all that is who chose for our sakes to become incarnate in Jesus.

We need to have church school classes devoted to this topic. We would do well to set up dialogue groups with Jews and Muslims to explore what it means to have one God of us all. We need to be sensitive to the realm of politics to avoid when possible legislation that builds walls between the church and others under the pretense of "protecting" the faith.

We have to find ways to talk about God's dismay and disappointment. God continues to experience pain when humans disregard or disobey divine instruction designed for our well-being. Jeremiah recognized this and shared in God's pain. Accepting that we have brought pain to others may do more to bring us to repentance than threats of punishment. To believe that our disobedience actually brings pain to God should be a revelation!

While there are indeed actions on the part of government, industry, and willful individuals that justify harsh criticism and call for repentance (as Jeremiah clearly reminds us), often there are other ways to express divine concern. For instance, concerning the complex problems of immigration, scolding and condemnation may be in order, but reaching out to care directly for all those affected is also needed. God knows the pain of the immigrants as well as the discomfort of those assigned the task of enforcing policies they have not formulated. The church has to stand with both groups, assuring all of God's love. The difficulty has been created by humans and must be rectified by humans. Nonetheless, all the dislocation and physical harm that have occurred have pained God. Rather than pounding the guilty with chastisement, the church needs to reach out, showing God's care and work to bring harmony out of chaos.

Finding ways to turn the discussion away from punishment to seeking reconciliation and renewal will be difficult. Central to such considerations should be the recognition that God is not nearly so "angry" at us as dismayed by us.

For Reflection and Action

1. Consider what it means that human behavior can bring pain to God. How might that view be communicated to the church? To the society? Suggest several ways to approach this subject with others in your congregation.

2. List ways other people or government policies bring pain to you. Share your list with others in your class. Which are the most commonly noted?

3. Have you experienced pain recently? When? How? Have you treated others in ways that might make them feel pain? What needs to change? How?

4. Discuss the difference between being punished because God is offended and because God is disappointed. How does your perception of punishment change if what happens is the warned result of failing to follow God's way? Does gravity make us fall, or is falling the negative result of ignoring or challenging gravity?

The ultimate test of a prophet's veracity was whether things happened as the prophet declared, but that takes time.

Chapter 5

Discerning Truth in the Midst of Turmoil

Scripture
Jeremiah 28:1–17   The prophet Hananiah prophesies peace and dies.

Jeremiah 29:1–23   Jeremiah writes a letter to the exiles in Babylon.

Prayer
O God, our Judge and Redeemer, you know full well the difficulties that surround your servants. Day by day new challenges arise. Obstacles hinder the way. Shortcuts to bypass your way tempt us. Help us to keep our eyes fixed on you, trusting in your love and grace. Hear our prayer, O God, for Jesus' sake. Amen.

Introduction
The years between 597 and 585 BCE in Mesopotamia in general, and Judah in particular, were tumultuous. Assyria's long dominance in Mesopotamia was over, and that brought the end to a period of relative (though at times harsh) stability in the region. Babylon succeeded in displacing Assyria as the dominant power. All the smaller countries, like Judah, were made Babylonian vassals and were expected to pay enormous tribute to Babylon.

Egypt, however, remained independent of Assyrian rule. The area now occupied by Palestine, Israel, Lebanon, and Syria served as a buffer between the southern reach of Babylon and the northern

31

edge of Egypt. Consequently, Egypt was continually trying to stir up Babylon's vassals, encouraging them to revolt and join Egypt.

In this period Babylon attacked her rebellious vassals in the west three times. Each military expedition resulted in large numbers of the local populations fleeing or being taken as exiles to various parts of the Babylonian empire. Obviously, this was disconcerting to those who were deported or who otherwise suffered the loss of their homes.

References to the experiences of some of the exiles from Judah allow a glimpse into what life in a foreign land, in a foreign culture, could be like. The exiles tended to live together in small communities and tried to stay in touch with their friends and relatives left behind in Judah. Letters were exchanged by way of various travelers.

Some exiles sought to maintain as much of their traditional culture as they could. Some of the same family and societal structures were preserved. Along with the Mosaic traditions, many of the psalms and some of the prophetic oracles and teachings, like those of Jeremiah, were being collected and preserved. And individuals were speaking in the name of God, claiming to be authentic prophets declaring new messages for the exiles to heed.

The passages to be considered in this chapter give us some understanding of the turmoil within which the exiles lived and the clashing of announcements that various "prophets" made with the words of Jeremiah. God's way was not always obvious.

A Basic Theme: Prophetic Words Take Time to Verify
The Babylonian exile posed two distinct choices for living in a foreign setting:

Go along to get along. One could merely give up regarding any commitment to the God of Moses and Jeremiah. Adjust to the ways of the Babylonians and move on. Indeed, many people did just that and were assimilated into Babylonian society. They gave up any allegiance to the God of Moses and to Jeremiah.

Stay the course. On the other hand, one could try to maintain belief in the God of Moses and Jeremiah and fashion a new community around this tradition. Many parts of the tradition had traveled with the people as they were relocated. They might have to be adjusted since temple worship was no longer possible, but adjustments were possible.

Adding energy to the whole enterprise was the presence of various "prophets" declaring God's will for these displaced folk. Illustrative of the disagreement among the prophets is the clash between Hananiah and Jeremiah among folk still in Jerusalem. While Jeremiah cautioned against the revolt, others spoke differently and prevailed. The Babylonians did, in fact, launch a successful attack that resulted in many people being taken as captives to Babylon. Still, prophets like Hananiah assured the people that peace would soon return (28:1–11). Jeremiah saw things differently and wore a yoke around his neck to symbolize Babylonian rule. Eventually, Jeremiah rebuked Hananiah and announced his coming death (28:15–17).

The problem for the people was that these events didn't follow quickly one after the other. Deuteronomy had set the test for evaluating a prophet. A true prophet will speak only in the Lord's name, and the word spoken will take place (Deuteronomy 18:21–22). Jeremiah had spoken in the Lord's name, but years and years passed, and his oracles against the king and Jerusalem had not happened. So why should he be believed? The event with Hananiah was one piece of evidence that Jeremiah's was the proper voice to heed.

Jeremiah sent a letter to those exiled in Babylon. It had at least two purposes:

Discredit false prophets. Jeremiah wanted to contend against false prophets who were telling the people that everything would soon be all right. The words of such false prophets would come to nothing because they were not from God (29:8–9).

Get used to your new home. Jeremiah's word from God instructed the people to settle in for the long hall. They were going to be there for a while. They were to build houses, plant, marry, make the most of what they had (29:5–6). They were even to pray for Babylon, the great enemy. Their welfare was connected to that of Babylon (29:7). Jeremiah gave the exiles a reason to hope: "I know the plans I have for you, says the Lord, plans for your welfare and not for harm, to give you a future with hope" (29:11). Thankfully, some followed Jeremiah's counsel. They did settle in and provided a model to follow by listening carefully and patiently for God's word.

The Life of Faith: A Balancing Act

The life of faith is seldom smooth. "Potholes" and unexpected obstacles appear right in the middle of the road. Illness comes, people die (some all too soon), jobs are lost, drug epidemics occur, and so on. In Jeremiah's time, people were ripped from their homes and their homeland and resettled in strange places surrounded by people who spoke a different language. Such things bring turmoil and uncertainty along with a challenge to any previous expectations one might have had concerning God.

So what do you do?

Keep on living. Day by day you get up and continue with the routine that is your life. You may not feel like it, but that will eventually pass.

Make adjustments. After some weeks of considering what has happened—a temporary setback or the permanent loss of a life partner—you realize that you can no longer linger over that second cup of coffee or assume that you will have the energy you have previously had to see you through. What are the truly essential things in your life that should be maintained? What can be removed? What can be traded?

Connect with your community or communities. Who are the people who energize you? With whom can you share an occasional "secret"? What activities interest you? (If you strike out on all fronts, get some professional help to help you recognize presently unrecognized opportunities.)

So far these are merely plain-sense suggestions that anyone might follow. But for the life of faith there is another essential step:

Consider what you really do believe. What can you hold on to when times get rough? For Jeremiah faith in God was a given, but the purposes of God were debated. Some contended that

God was punishing them for their faithlessness, and indeed some of what Jeremiah had pronounced supported such a view. Many today consider personal problems to be punishment for past or present wrongdoings by them personally or by the nation.

Jeremiah, however, had a new word for the exiles. Yes, they needed to go about life in many of the ways they regularly did, but they needed one more word to see them on their way. Jeremiah was convinced that God's intentions for them were good, not evil. Despite how things looked at any given moment, they were to live in the confidence that God was for them, not against them.

We have to take stock of our own faith convictions. The gospel of Jesus Christ is part of our heritage—thank God! We are not to pretend life is a bed of roses, but neither are we to lose sight of God's intentions for good. Healthy skepticism about "easy answers," quick "political fixes," or "pie in the sky" theologies is required. But this must be kept in balance with solid trust in the goodness of our Judge and Redeemer.

The Church: Commitment in the Midst of Turmoil

Our world is in the midst of turmoil as was Jeremiah's. Political strife is rampant. For many, military solutions seem to be the answer. Economies seem fragile. Some are becoming extraordinarily wealthy while many more remain quite vulnerable to changes in the job market or the climate. Personal ethical behavior among our leaders is increasingly problematic. Church membership is in severe decline. Things are bad and show no signs of improving.

What can we do?

The church needs to recognize and acknowledge its "minority" status. The church began with twelve and might well have stayed small and mobile were it not for a Roman emperor named Constantine who "converted" and declared all his subjects to be "Christians." Political changes suddenly made thousands and thousands "Christian" with little understanding of what that should mean regarding a way of life. Over the past fifty years, church membership, after dramatic growth in the 1950s, has been on the decline in Europe and the United States. There may have been a time when the majority of folk were active in the church, but that is no longer the case. The church can no longer (if ever it could) merely tell the wider society how to live and expect that to happen.

The church needs to concentrate on creating and/or maintaining communities of faith. Small groups of people working together toward common goals while offering support to one another have proven effective. This is true in many small towns and small congregations. The emphasis should not be on increasing membership rolls but rather on assisting growth and well-being within the group and those with whom the group may have contact (e.g., older folk, the schools, the hospitals, etc.). To help smaller and larger communities flourish is the current task.

The church needs to demonstrate what commitment means for individuals and groups. Many do not seem to understand any longer what "commitment" is all about. Marriages collapse all too soon because of an unwillingness to do the demanding work of commitment with one another. Too many businesses and organizations are led by people who seem to think only of themselves. "What's in it for me?" seems to be the motivation of many, with little regard for those other than "me."

Faith communities need to demonstrate what caring for one another is all about. Not all marriages should continue, but there should be adequate help and encouragement provided by the church to assist in making loving decisions. Leadership in the church on its boards and committees should demonstrate commitment in the way various people are brought into the process of decision making. Democracy is not always efficient or quick, but it is the best way we have fashioned so far to build and maintain communities. The church should highlight democracy as a value to be cherished and defended.

For Reflection and Action

1. Share some occasions where you as an individual or congregation have experienced what it means that God's purpose for you includes your welfare. How might these incidents be communicated to the larger group(s) within which you operate?

2. How can "prophets" be evaluated today? What does it mean when things go differently from what a "prophet" proclaims? Are all "prophets" to be judged by the same standard?

3. Does the Bible count as a witness to the validity of a contemporary "prophet"? Read 1 Corinthians 13, and relate it to the consideration of "true" prophecy.

4. Consider your own congregation or community in terms of a place where an expression and example of commitment might be helpful. Try to imagine ways to provide such, and then plan to do so.

Though Jeremiah declared grave news, that was not his only word. Destruction, plucking up, was to come but so were building and planting. God's work was not over.

Chapter 6

God's Ongoing Plan: A New Covenant

Scripture

Jeremiah 30:10–24 Through Jeremiah, God promises restoration to Israel and Judah.

Jeremiah 31:27–37 God will make a new covenant with Israel and Judah and write it on their hearts.

Prayer

O God of hope, continue to assure us of your loving care. When we get despondent, grant that we may see the world as you do with all its possibilities. When a sense of futility and defeat captures us, free us that we may claim with enthusiasm and conviction the opportunities that you offer. You are creating a new world! Help us to participate in your glorious work. In Jesus' name we pray. Amen.

Introduction

Chapters 30–31 of Jeremiah have been named the "Book of Consolation." Many scholars think that these chapters circulated independently before being added to Jeremiah in the process of fashioning the book as we have it. Other material associated with Jeremiah (though not likely his own words) was brought together at about the same time and preserved as the book of Lamentations.

The central part of the Book of Consolation consists of 30:5–31:22. The introductory material (30:1–4) and the three

39

concluding prose oracles (31:27–37) provide an envelope for the older poetic sections. If Jeremiah created the central material, he did so in his early years because it is all directed at Israel, the Northern Kingdom, which fell to the Assyrians in 721 BCE. This chapter will consider a portion of the central material and one of the concluding oracles. The material "added" to the final form of Jeremiah puts the prophet's whole message into an appropriate frame.

The central part of the Book of Consolation acknowledges that the Northern Kingdom has been destroyed in punishment and scattered in exile. But the people will be redeemed and brought back to their homeland (30:10–11; 18–22). While these may or may not be Jeremiah's words, they fit his theology. God does punish, but God does not forsake. God yet has a purpose for the reunited Israel and Judah to serve.

Further, Jeremiah envisions that God intends a "new covenant." A covenant is a legal agreement that defines relationships between those who accept it. God's new covenant is a continuation of the Mosaic covenant fashioned at Sinai, but with some significant new features. There is no certain way to determine whether this is original to Jeremiah, but it also fits well with his theology.

The Bible's authority does not depend on our knowledge of who wrote it, but rather on the Spirit. The authority is there because of the Spirit that inspired the speakers/writers and those who collected and preserved their words. It is to them and the God who directed the process that we owe profound thanks for a guidepost that leads us on our way.

A Basic Theme: God's Restoration of Hope
There is an important message in this material. God acknowledges that Jacob (i.e., the Northern Kingdom Israel) has been dealt with quite severely, utterly destroyed by the Assyrians (30:12–15)! They were punished for their sinfulness. But the story doesn't end there; God intends to restore Israel. God will exercise compassion so that there may be restoration. The land will be filled with joyous celebration, honor, and all that goes with being a vital country protected by God (30:18–21). Then God, using the traditional covenant formula, announces, "And you shall be my people, and I will be your God" (30:22; see 7:23; 11:4).

The hope God extends, however, as far as the context is concerned, is entirely in the future. Israel has not yet been restored. God declares that it will be, but there is no evidence at this point to use to convince Jeremiah's audience. God says it will happen, and that has to be enough! God's commitment to Israel and Judah is Jeremiah's explanation for both their punishment and their restoration. God's faithfulness is the foundation for accepting Jeremiah's inaugural commission, the declaration that there would be both uprooting and planting (1:10).

Numerous expressions of God's intention to forgive and restore are found in the Book of Consolation, but toward the end is a prose oracle that articulates some of how this will come about. God's instrument of reclamation will be a new covenant that God will establish with Israel-Judah. The "old covenant" was good and should have been sufficient, but the people—not God—broke it and went away from God (31:32).

For any covenant to be maintained by humans there needed to be a new guidance system. Their "hearts" (in Hebrew psychology the "heart" was the seat of the "will") had let the people down. Thus God would write the new law on their hearts, not on stone tablets. The people then would be capable of knowing God (31:33). A further expansion reads, "I will give them one heart and one way, that they may fear [i.e., "honor"] me for all time, for their own good and the good of their children after them" (32:39). The prophet Ezekiel expressed somewhat the same idea when he declared that God intended to remove from the people their "heart of stone" and replace it with "a heart of flesh" and a "new spirit" (Ezekiel 36:26–27). Then all would "know" the Lord and would not need instruction (31:34). Moreover, the new covenant was guaranteed: it would not be dependent on human obedience but rather on divine forgiveness (31:34).

This offer of a new covenant was extravagant! It made possible a new beginning for God and the people. The hope it created would always be available because God's forgiveness was the promised basis. Further, this hope, this new covenant, did not require human affirmation. It was offered merely as a divine gift, a gracious divine gift!

The Life of Faith: Accepting God's Gift of Hope

There is an old adage about advertising: If something looks too good to be true, then it probably is. Unconditional forgiveness certainly seems like something too good to be true. Still, for others, God's mercy doesn't matter anyway. They are just not interested; they don't think they need forgiveness.

To accept God's gracious gift at least two things are immediately necessary: 1) belief that there is a God and 2) the recognition of how seriously one has disappointed (sinned against) God. If those two things are missing, then the conversation need go no further. But if the belief in God and the recognition of sin are present, then Jeremiah's proclamation is significant.

What does it mean to have our rebellions excused, erased, wiped out? Among other things, it means that each new day is indeed a new day. Past failures and wrongdoings need no longer weigh one down. They need to be recognized and acknowledged as our own doing, but then we can move on. God invites us into a relationship based on divine forgiveness, not one waiting to be found. Forgiveness is real, unending, renewing!

This seems wonderful, but it is not quite as easy as it might sound. Reluctance can get in the way, not God's but ours. Many people will not readily admit to making errors in judgment or deliberately breaking the rules. If you have lived a long time thinking (because someone told you) that black cats bring bad luck, then it will be tough to like the neighbor's new black cat. Or if an unscrupulous merchant has cheated you, then it will be challenging to trust another. Or if you have been taught that "white" people are better than "colored" people, then it will be difficult for you to function justly as an admissions director at your local school. It is difficult to believe that God can and will just forgive our trespasses because we have long been taught that we have to earn God's love and favor by being "good." Jeremiah says otherwise and invites a different approach to life.

To the degree that we accept his pronouncement, two things can happen. We have already talked about living in forgiveness. The other is learning to live in hope. Things can be different. A lost job doesn't have to be the end of the world. Bad policies adopted by governments can be changed. Living with God-given hope enables the recognition of new possibilities. Yes, there are dead-end roads, but not all roads will automatically be such. Detours are always possible if hope is a lively ingredient in our planning.

God offers us hope, but only we can accept it and live in it. Participating in a community of faith can make a serious difference. We need one another to remind us that God has already forgiven us and offered us the wonderful gift of hope.

The Church: A Message of Restorative Hope

Things certainly look bad in our world. Wars continue. Refugees and immigrants desperately seek refuge. Economic rivalries grow intense. Populations in the urbanized world are aging. Health programs are losing necessary funding. The world climate is changing. Alliances among nations seem to be falling apart. And nothing much seems to be happening in response! We are in somewhat the same state that Jeremiah's Judah found itself. Things were in a total mess. So what was Jeremiah's final word? Have confidence in the restorative love of God.

That message is what the church has to share. It may seem meaningless when the means to enable it seem so absent. Those taken away in exile to Babylon thought all hope was lost. Centuries later the disciples who watched while Jesus was crucified indeed thought the end had come. Hard times have repeatedly come, but again and again hope has won out, and new people and new churches and new governments and new economies have come forth. This may merely be the result of "natural" forces, but those of faith keep on assigning such "miracles" of restoration to the will and power of God.

The task of the church now is to keep urging people to hope and work toward that new world God intends. Though it is difficult sometimes to keep going, that is precisely what we are called to do. Injustice seems so widely spread, power so unequally shared, that, as the saying goes, the rich get richer, and the poor get poorer. But this is not the way God desires. So it is ours to keep reminding all those around us, as well as one another, that things can change and that a new order will eventually prevail.

There are actions we can take to demonstrate our convictions. We can agitate for change in governmental policy. We know we probably will not win the battle today, but we might tomorrow. We can support programs that are aimed at assisting the poor: food pantries, lunch programs, housing repairs, aids for the homeless, health clinics, foster care for needful children, programs of care for the aging, and so on and on. There is much to be done. Even seemingly unimportant things are significant because each one is a declaration that things are not right, that restorative justice is needed, and that some folk hope and believe that such things are possible.

A hymn expresses well what this is all about, "Live Into Hope"[1] by Jane Parker Huber (verses 1 and 4):

> Live into hope of captives freed.
> Of sight regained, the end of greed.
> The oppressed shall be the first to see
> The Year of God's own jubilee.
>
> Live into hope of captives freed
> From chains of fear or want or greed.
> God now proclaims our full release
> To faith and hope and joy and peace.

This is our task and message.

For Reflection and Action

1. Genuine hoping is different from merely wishing. Hope triggers expectation and expectation produces action. What kind of expectations and actions does trusting that God's work of restoration is ongoing produce? How might you and your church contribute to God's work?

2. List some of the ways that Judah's tumultuous situation in Jeremiah's time seems similar to that we experience now.

---

1. © Jane Parker Huber from *A Singing Faith* (Philadelphia: Westminster Press, 1987).

3. What are some concrete ways of helping others (as well as yourself) really accept God's forgiveness and put aside old fears and self-criticism?

4. Reflect on Parker's hymn and sketch out other ways to "live into hope." Consider some practical steps you and your congregation might take to move forward more intentionally toward hope.

Group Gatherings

Mark D. Hinds

Jeremiah: A Prophet like Moses

Main Idea

Jeremiah demonstrates what it can mean to be embraced by God and claimed for special service. All believers can find comfort and strength in recognizing how God will in fact sustain and guide them. To receive a sense of purpose is a great gift amid the uncertainties of our present world.

Preparing to Lead

- Read and reflect on chapter 1, "Jeremiah: A Prophet like Moses."
- Review this plan for the group gathering, and select questions and activities that you will use.
- What other questions, issues, or themes occur to you from your reflection?

Gathering

- Provide name tags and pens as people arrive.
- Provide simple refreshments; ask volunteers to bring refreshments for the next five gatherings.
- Agree on simple ground rules and organization (for example, time to begin and end; location for gatherings; welcoming of all points of view; confidentiality; and so on). Encourage participants to bring their study books and Bibles.

Opening Worship

Prayer (unison)

O awesome God, you have sought us across the centuries, inviting us into relationship with you. You have come to us in the person of prophets, in mighty acts of deliverance, and, finally, in the person of your Son Jesus, our Lord. Still we are often uncertain of your will. Help us now as we study the book of your prophet Jeremiah to gain the insight and perspective we need to live in the way you desire and relish. For Jesus' sake, hear our prayer. Amen.

Prayerful, Reflective Reading
- Read Deuteronomy 18:15–22 aloud.
- Invite all to reflect for a few minutes in silence.
- After reflection time, invite all to listen for a word or phrase as the passage is read again and to reflect on that word or phrase in silence.
- Read the passage a third time, asking all to offer a silent prayer following the reading.
- Invite volunteers to share the word or phrase that spoke most deeply to them.

Prayer
Loving God, hear our prayers today as we seek to follow you more faithfully:

(*spoken prayers may be offered*)

Hear us now as we pray together, saying, Our Father . . .

Conversation
- Introduce chapter 1, "Jeremiah: A Prophet like Moses." Share observations, reflections, and insights.
- Review the Introduction (pp. 1–2). Share these key points:
  a. Jeremiah the prophet was active between the years 609 BCE and 585 BCE, witnessing and interpreting the fall of Judah to the Babylonians, including the exile of large numbers of Judean leaders to Babylon.
  b. The book of Jeremiah is closely related to parts of the book of Deuteronomy, which insists that the proper foundation for Israel's relationship with God is the Mosaic covenant.
  c. Only a few are claimed by God for the work of being a prophet, a *nabi'*. Jeremiah is compared with Moses in terms of the divine call.
  d. Biblical prophets did not make predictions about the future. They announced God's will for the present! That is how the book of Jeremiah is to be heard and understood.

Challenge the participants to recall and name features of the Mosaic covenant (e.g. God establishes a relationship based on God's character of steadfast love and justice, and God calls the people to live by the Ten Commandments, prohibiting idolatry).

- Review "A Basic Theme: Appointed over Nations and Kingdoms" (pp. 2–3). Share these key points:
  a. God called Jeremiah, like Moses, to confront his king and his people in a very harsh way with their idolatry and immorality (i.e., Pharaoh in Egypt and a vassal puppet king in Judah).
  b. Because of widespread idolatry (1:16), Jeremiah was certain of a coming judgment.
  c. Even though Jeremiah has been seen as a negative person with no good news to share, a time "to build and to plant" was also part of God's word for Jeremiah to declare (1:10).

Discuss the challenges Jeremiah faced in proclaiming a harsh word from God to the rulers and the people. Ask:

What assurance did Jeremiah have that God would be with him during his ministry (1:8, 19)?

If Jeremiah were alive today, to whom would he address his word from the Lord? Why?

- Review "The Life of Faith: Being Embraced by a Loving God" (pp. 3–4). Discuss the story of Jeremiah's call to ministry as an account of being embraced by a loving God. Invite the participants to share stories of how God has embraced them.

In what ways do you embrace having been embraced by a loving God?

Have you been claimed for special service? What difference does a sense of purpose add to your life?

What comfort and strength do you find in recognizing that God sustains and guides you? How is God's presence discernible in your life?

- Review "The Church: Living Out Jeremiah's Call" (pp. 5–6). Share these key points:
  a. A fundamental realignment of the church's priorities needs to be made. The goal is not to expand the church (though that may at times occur). The goal is to engage the "nations." The church has a very difficult challenge: to show why theology and politics should not be separated.
  b. Our society's economic structure that rewards acquisition is in dire need of attention.
  c. The recognition that God is sovereign over all kingdoms and nations is often denied directly or indirectly.

Discuss the resistance that most have to the notion that faith and religion can legitimately address the political and economic sectors of our society. Brainstorm ways to correct this. Ask:

Jeremiah's commission was to address the "nations," not just individuals and certainly not only "spiritual" matters. In what ways does the church accept Jeremiah's commission today?

What are some appropriate ways for the church to engage in political action? Are there inappropriate ways? What are they?

Are there prophets among us today? Who are they, and how are they addressing the problems of idolatry and social justice?

Conclusion
Read Jeremiah 1:4–19 and Romans 13:1–10. Invite the participants to compare the texts, as suggested in the fourth question in For Reflection and Action (p. 6). Ask them to reflect during the week on how Romans 13:8–10 influences their reading of Jeremiah.

Passing the Peace
The peace of Christ be with you.
    And also with you.
Amen.

The Angry Dismay of God

Main Idea
The basic issue is how to understand and appreciate the so-called "wrath" of God. Jeremiah presents God's "anger" as springing from God's dismay and disappointment over the disobedience of the Judean king and people. God's dismay is not irrational.

Preparing to Lead
- Read and reflect on chapter 2, "The Angry Dismay of God."
- Review this plan for the group gathering, and select questions and activities that you will use.
- What other questions, issues, or themes occur to you from your reflection?

Gathering
- Provide simple refreshments as people arrive and name tags if needed.

Opening Worship
Prayer (unison)
Gracious God, patient God, enable us to recognize and acknowledge when our behavior brings dismay and anger to you. Help us to turn from such action and make a more determined effort to do your will. We desire to please you and honor you. Guide us, and strengthen us in our efforts. Hear our prayer for Jesus' sake. Amen.

Prayerful, Reflective Reading
- Read Jeremiah 3:1–5a aloud.
- Invite all to reflect for a few minutes in silence.

- After reflection time, invite all to listen for a word or phrase as the passage is read again and to reflect on that word or phrase in silence.
- Read the passage a third time, asking all to offer a silent prayer following the reading.
- Invite volunteers to share the word or phrase that spoke most deeply to them.

Prayer

Loving God, hear our prayers today as we seek to follow you more faithfully:

(*spoken prayers may be offered*)

Hear us now as we pray together, saying, Our Father . . .

Conversation

- Introduce chapter 2, "The Angry Dismay of God." Share observations, reflections, and insights.
- Review the Introduction (pp. 7–8). Share these key points:
  a. Chapter 2 deals with two broad sections of the book of Jeremiah, 2–25 and 26–51, that emphasize that Jeremiah was called to address the nations.
  b. The first section consists, largely though not totally, of oracles of judgment announced against the Judean king and people.
  c. The second section presents a number of oracles against neighboring nations, some of which are exercising rule over Judah, or have done so in the past.
- Review "A Basic Theme: The Reality of Divine Dismay" (pp. 8–10). Share these key points:
  a. God is deeply troubled by the people of Judah.
  b. God brought the people out of Egypt through the wilderness into a fruitful land. Once there, the people and their leaders went after other deities. In so doing they violated the covenant oaths they had taken at Sinai.
  c. Divine dismay at the actions of the people has led to God's anger.

Have the participants skim Jeremiah 2–25 and 26–51 in their Bibles, noting the names of nations and their sins. Ask:

Judah's idolatry is characterized as adultery and whoredom. In what way is this a fitting characterization?

Moab did not break a covenant with God. How would you describe Moab's sin?

How do you imagine the rulers and citizens of the nations reacted to Jeremiah's oracles of judgment?

Is God's anger warranted? Why?

What are some of the ways to "explain" or "unpack" the difficulty of acknowledging that God can become angry?

• Review "The Life of Faith: Acknowledging the Reality of Divine Anger" (pp. 10–11). Share these key points:
  a. One of the most challenging faith issues to deal with is the matter of God's anger. We have been taught that anger is bad, wrong, and "ungodly."
  b. The Bible does not speak of God as "impassable," impossible to engage emotion, or unable to suffer.
  c. God can love and yet be disappointed.
  Discuss the notion that when we do harm to one another, we anger God. Ask:

Do you agree that if God can't get angry, then God cannot love either? Why? Why not?

How does an angry God fit your personal belief system?

What breaks God's heart?

• Review "The Church: Announcing God's Displeasure" (pp. 11–12). Share these key points:
  a. A primary task of the church today is declaring the grave displeasure God has with the manner in which people are treated, individually and as groups.
  b. The church must choose to "meddle" where it thinks the most can be done, using these efforts as signals to point to all that needs reform.

Name problems in your community or country that Jeremiah might consider displeasing to God. Do the problems rise to the level of idolatry or covenant breaking? Why? Why not?

Replace the names of ancient nations in Jeremiah 2–25 and 26–51 with the names of present-day nations, such as the United States and its surrounding nations. How do you react to hearing God's judgment against your homeland?

In what ways should the church convey God's anger and dismay?

Ask a volunteer to read Luke 11:37–54. Discuss how Jeremiah supports Luke's presentation of Jesus, as suggested in the first question in For Reflection and Action (pp. 12–13). Ask:

How can we be good citizens of our nation and maintain sole allegiance to God?

Do Jesus' words in Luke 11:37–54 help or confuse the issue?

Conclusion
Invite the group to name a particular matter of injustice or need in your local area. Develop a plan of action to address the need.

Passing the Peace
The peace of Christ be with you.
     And also with you.
Amen.

The Mosaic Way Is God's Desired Way

Main Idea

The basic theme concerns the breakdown of the influence of the Mosaic covenant. Individual immorality as well as the disruption of social norms appear. As viewed through the Mosaic covenant, the rampant forms of idolatry found in contemporary society are signs of extreme danger. Challenging these "false gods" is necessary but should not be seen as a way to gain God's love and forgiveness. God's gracious mercy is God's doing and is freely given.

Preparing to Lead

- Read and reflect on chapter 3, "The Mosaic Way Is God's Desired Way."
- Review this plan for the group session, and select questions and activities that you will use.
- Gather newsprint and markers, if needed, and prepare to post newsprint sheets on a wall or bulletin board.
- Create a simple timeline on a large sheet of paper. Include the following dates and events:
    620 BCE: A scroll found in the Temple
    609: Josiah dies
    609–585: Jeremiah's ministry
    605: Jeremiah's sermon
    597, 587, 585: Babylon attacks Judah
- What other questions, issues, or themes occur to you from your reflection?

Gathering

- Provide simple refreshments as people arrive and name tags if needed.

Opening Worship
Prayer (unison)
O God of the prophets, continue to guide us. We are grateful for the prophets you have sent. We know we are stubborn and inattentive. Enable us to hear them and to follow your instruction. Provide us with the eyes to see and ears to hear your word. In Jesus' name we pray. Amen.

Prayerful, Reflective Reading
- Read Jeremiah 7:1–15 aloud.
- Invite all to reflect for a few minutes in silence.
- After reflection time, invite all to listen for a word or phrase as the passage is read again and to reflect on that word or phrase in silence.
- Read the passage a third time, asking all to offer a silent prayer following the reading.
- Invite volunteers to share the word or phrase that spoke most deeply to them.

Prayer
Loving God, hear our prayers today as we seek to follow you more faithfully:

(*spoken prayers may be offered*)

Hear us now as we pray together, saying, Our Father . . .

Conversation
- Introduce chapter 3, "The Mosaic Way Is God's Desired Way." Share observations, reflections, and insights.
- Display the large sheet of paper with the timeline you created. Review the history behind chapter 3:
  a. In 620 a scroll was found in the Temple in Jerusalem (2 Kings 22). The content of the scroll prompted King Josiah to conduct a thorough reform, removing all the idols and other signs of idolatrous worship in Judah (2 Kings 23).
  b. Many scholars believe that the scroll was an early version of the book of Deuteronomy.
  c. Explain that when Josiah died in 609, reform was set aside, and the people turned back to the idolatry they had practiced previously.

d. The beginning of Jeremiah's ministry coincides with Josiah's death and his successor's decision to suspend reform, and it ends when Babylon finally destroys Judah (609–585 BCE).

e. Three times Judean leaders were exiled to Babylonia (597, 587, 585 BCE). The rightful king was replaced with a "puppet" appointed by and loyal to Babylon.

f. War had continued to ravage the nation. The economy was in bad shape. Religion was profoundly messed up. There was a great fear among the people and very little hope that things could be righted.

- Review "A Basic Theme: God's Preference for the Mosaic Way" (pp. 16–17). Share these key points:

a. In 605 Jeremiah addressed the people at the Temple, lambasting them and their new king for rejecting the teaching of the Mosaic covenant.

b. Jeremiah declared a disaster was about to fall on Judah: the destruction of the land and the Temple.

c. This "sermon" is reported in Jeremiah 7 with a description of the outcome in Jeremiah 26.

Invite volunteers to skim and summarize Jeremiah 7 and 26. Discuss the competing ideologies apparent in the text: the Mosaic covenant, centered in the Passover and the Ten Commandments, and the Davidic covenant, the royal ideology that assured the people of God's protection of the Temple and the Davidic king.

Since both covenants are biblical, how do we interpret Jeremiah's condemnation of the people's rejecting the Mosaic covenant and putting their faith in the Davidic covenant (i.e., royal lineage and the Temple)?

Jeremiah emphasizes the "Love God, love your neighbor as yourself" ethic of the Mosaic covenant. Is there a danger in putting our trust in doing the right thing?

Name some of the "false gods" that you see in our society. How do they affect our national life? Your personal life?

What are some of the differences in what some call our national "values" and what Jeremiah understood as the Mosaic way?

- Review "The Life of Faith: Seeking to Live in God's Way" (pp. 18–19). Share these three essential motifs for living in God's way:
  a. The Lord alone is worthy of worship. Idolatry is absolutely forbidden!
  b. Personal behavior matters. The Ten Commandments are crucial for a healthy community.
  c. Our relationship with God is finally and entirely dependent upon God.

  Help participants understand the danger of idolatry. A false god is anything or anyone who claims our absolute allegiance. To begin a discussion on this potentially sensitive topic, be vulnerable: Name ways that you are compromised by allegiance to a variety of idols, and invite the group to follow your lead. Seek ways to illustrate how idolatries are toxic. Discuss:

  How can living by the Ten Commandments in the assurance of God's grace and mercy help stave off idolatry in your life?

- Review "The Church: A Time to Speak Out" (pp. 19–20). Remind the group that modern prophets also attempt to read the signs of our times in light of their convictions about what God wants for God's people. Then read to the group the following contemporary prophetic statements that conflict with one another. Ask them to decide which reflect Jeremiah's prophetic themes.

  Christians must care for the earth and its resources and live in harmony with God's creation.

  God is Spirit; therefore, Christians must focus on eternal spiritual concerns, not temporary earthly affairs.

  God despises your fancy electronic toys, your designer kitchens, and your $100 shoes while the poor of the world have little to eat and nowhere to live.

  Wealthy Christian consumers are creating jobs for people all over the world who would not have them otherwise. A world consumer economy will bring dignity to all the world's citizens.

America is being destroyed by the goals of prosperity at any price, peace at any price, safety first instead of duty first, and love of soft living and the get-rich-quick theory of life.

My country is better than yours. My country is the greatest there has ever been. They hate my country because it is so good.

- Brainstorm several idols that the church should address today. If not mentioned, raise false nationalism as a dangerous idol for our country overall. National pride is not bad, but when it is touted as all important, it begins to rival God, and that is wrong. Discuss:

  In what ways can the church aid, support, or correct those caught up in the conflict over national policies that challenge the right to disagree with the national government?

Conclusion

Choose a contemporary idol that seems of greatest concern to the participants. Ask what resources, persons, and practices they may employ to clarify their understandings. Encourage them to be specific. Ask:

How difficult is it to name contemporary idolatries?

What questions about the named idolatry would you bring to Scripture, tradition, families, pastors, experts, and other leaders?

What practices might you adopt that could inform your understanding of the idol?

What do you risk by taking a stand? By not taking a stand?

Passing the Peace

The peace of Christ be with you.
    And also with you.
Amen.

Sharing God's Frustration and Pain

Main Idea
God is capable of experiencing pain. God's pain comes from dismay and disappointment provoked by human disobedience. Jeremiah shared God's pain, and so must we. Recognizing and accepting the reality of God's pain are critical prerequisites for turning away from the behavior that causes that pain.

Preparing to Lead
- Read and reflect on chapter 4, "Sharing God's Frustration and Pain."
- Review this plan for the group gathering, and select questions and activities that you will use.
- What other questions, issues, or themes occur to you from your reflection?

Gathering
- Provide simple refreshments as people arrive and name tags if needed.

Opening Worship
Prayer (unison)
Merciful God, Jeremiah was acutely aware of the pain the disobedience of your people caused you. He shared your pain and your suffering. Grant that we may catch a glimpse of what you experience and join with Jeremiah in sharing some of that discomfort. Hear our prayer for we offer it through Jesus our Lord. Amen.

Prayerful, Reflective Reading
- Read Jeremiah 4:19–22 aloud.
- Invite all to reflect for a few minutes in silence.
- After reflection time, invite all to listen for a word or phrase as the passage is read again and to reflect on that word or phrase in silence.
- Read the passage a third time, asking all to offer a silent prayer following the reading.
- Invite volunteers to share the word or phrase that spoke most deeply to them.

Prayer
Loving God, hear our prayers today as we seek to follow you more faithfully:

(*spoken prayers may be offered*)

Hear us now as we pray together, saying, Our Father . . .

Conversation
- Introduce chapter 4, "Sharing God's Frustration and Pain." Share observations, reflections, and insights.
- Review the Introduction (pp. 23–24). Share these key points:
  a. The psalms contain numerous poems formerly called "laments" in commentaries that are now known as "complaints."
  b. Jeremiah includes a number of "supplications/complaints."
  c. Foundational to the complaint/supplication is the conviction that honest expression of negative feelings to God is not wrong.
  Invite the participants to name the feelings of God found in Jeremiah 2:29–32; 9:17–18; 12:7; and 31:2–3. Describe the suffering and anguish of God. Discuss the reasons for God's pain.
- Review "A Basic Theme: The Prophet Shares God's Pain" (pp. 24–26). Share these key points:
  a. God is frustrated by and very much in pain over Judah's behavior. Jeremiah knows and shares God's pain, but does not understand.

b. Jeremiah was also angry with God for giving him such an assignment. He accused God of having "enticed" (Hebrew, "seduced") him and "overpowered" him, forcing him to deliver God's painful message (20:7).

c. Nevertheless Jeremiah puts his confidence in God to surely bring vindication (17:9–11; 20:12).

Invite the participants to reflect on the difference between being "punished" because God is offended and because God is disappointed, as suggested in the fourth question in For Reflection and Action.

How does your perception of punishment change if what happens is the warned result of failing to follow God's way?

Does gravity make us fall, or is falling the negative result of ignoring or challenging gravity?

- Review "The Life of Faith: Recognizing and Responding to God's Pain" (pp. 26–27). Share these key points:

a. We have to understand that God experiences frustration and pain:

—Jeremiah testifies to the frustration and pain God experiences. Jeremiah's understanding of God belies the popular view that the Old Testament represents God as only wrathful, vengeful, and hateful.

—Jesus demonstrated God's pain over a wayward people (Luke 19:41–44) when he wept over Jerusalem.

b. We must claim our share of the pain known by God and repent or turn from the behavior that breaks God's heart.

c. Recognizing and sharing in God's pain can equip us to better accept who we are and to care for one another.

Discuss:

Have you experienced pain recently? When? How?

Have you treated others in ways that might make them feel pain?

What needs to change? How?

- Review "The Church: Sharing God's Dismay" (pp. 27–28). Share these key points:
  a. The church has presented a distorted view of the Old Testament; that God is only a God of judgment.
  b. This distortion has allowed the rise of anti-Jewish ideologies and a misunderstanding of Jesus' ministry.
  c. There are at least two ways to address this problem:
     —There needs to be a concerted effort in the church to correct the misinformation. There are not two "gods," one of the Old Testament—a wrathful deity—and a second of the New Testament—a gracious, forgiving deity.
     —We have to find ways to talk about God's dismay and disappointment. Accepting that we have brought pain to others may do more to bring us to repentance than threats of punishment. To believe that our disobedience brings pain to God should be a revelation!

Consider what it means that human behavior can bring pain to God. Discuss:

How do other people or government policies bring you pain?

How can you approach this subject with others in your congregation? In our society?

Conclusion

Brainstorm a variety of educational efforts to be developed at the local congregational level as well as in the wider community to counter anti-Jewish ideologies and to enable Christians to understand and share in God's pain. Share these with your church board or governing council.

Passing the Peace

The peace of Christ be with you.
   And also with you.
Amen.

Discerning Truth in the Midst of Turmoil

Main Idea

Jeremiah told the exiles to plan for an extended stay. Other voices gave conflicting advice. The difficulty was in discerning who was in fact speaking for God. The ultimate test of veracity was whether things happened as the prophet declared, but that takes time.

Preparing to Lead

- Read and reflect on chapter 5, "Discerning Truth in the Midst of Turmoil."
- Review this plan for the group gathering, and select questions and activities that you will use.
- What other questions, issues, or themes occur to you from your reflection?

Gathering

- Provide simple refreshments as people arrive and name tags if needed.

Opening Worship

Prayer (unison)

O God, our Judge and Redeemer, you know full well the difficulties that surround your servants. Day by day new challenges arise. Obstacles hinder the way. Shortcuts to bypass your way tempt us. Help us to keep our eyes fixed on you, trusting in your love and grace. Hear our prayer, O God, for Jesus' sake. Amen.

Prayerful, Reflective Reading

- Read Jeremiah 28:10–17 aloud.
- Invite all to reflect for a few minutes in silence.

- After reflection time, invite all to listen for a word or phrase as the passage is read again and to reflect on that word or phrase in silence.
- Read the passage a third time, asking all to offer a silent prayer following the reading.
- Invite volunteers to share the word or phrase that spoke most deeply to them.

Prayer

Loving God, hear our prayers today as we seek to follow you more faithfully:

(*spoken prayers may be offered*)

Hear us now as we pray together, saying, Our Father . . .

Conversation

- Introduce chapter 5, "Discerning Truth in the Midst of Turmoil." Share observations, reflections, and insights.
- Review the Introduction (pp. 31–32). Share these key points:
  a. Jeremiah lived in a time of turmoil. His time, as is ours, was marked by war and political upheaval.
  b. For the Judeans in exile there were two possibilities: to give up their heritage and be assimilated into Babylonian society or to settle in and do the best they could in a hostile environment.
- Review "A Basic Theme: Prophetic Words Take Time to Verify" (pp. 32–34). Share these key points:
  a. Complicating things for the exiles was the fact that there were conflicting voices rendering counsel. Some claiming to speak for God announced that things would soon get better. Jeremiah, on the other hand, told the exiles to plan for an extended stay.
  b. The difficulty was to discern who was in fact speaking for God. The ultimate test of veracity was whether things happened as the prophet declared, but that takes time.
  c. In the meantime, people have to do the best they can. For individuals that means sticking with tradition and adjusting as necessary.

Discuss:

> *How can "prophets" be evaluated today? What does it mean when things go differently from what a "prophet" proclaims? Are all "prophets" to be judged by the same standard?*
>
> *Does the Bible count as a witness to the validity of a contemporary "prophet"? Read 1 Corinthians 13, and relate it to the consideration of "true" prophecy.*

• Review "The Life of Faith: A Balancing Act" (pp. 34–35). Share these key points:
  a. In his letter to the exiles (29:1–23), Jeremiah sends God's advice on how to live in exile and warns them concerning false prophets.
  b. Jeremiah gives the exiles reason to hope, assuring them of God's good plans for the exiles after their return.
  Read aloud Jeremiah 29:10–14. Share some occasions where you have experienced what it means that God's purpose for you includes your welfare.

  Jeremiah was convinced that God's intentions for them were good, not evil. Despite how things looked at any given moment, they were to live in the confidence that God was for them, not against them. Discuss ways in which Jeremiah's counsel to the exiles offers hope to those living in turbulent times today.

• Review "The Church: Commitment in the Midst of Turmoil" (pp. 35–36). Share these key points:
  a. Our world is in the midst of turmoil as was Jeremiah's. Political strife is rampant. For many, military solutions seem to be the answer. Economies seem fragile. Some are becoming extraordinarily wealthy while many more remain quite vulnerable to changes in the job market or the climate. Personal ethical behavior among our leaders is increasingly problematic.
  b. The church needs to:
  —recognize and acknowledge its "minority" status.
  —concentrate on creating and/or maintaining communities of faith.

—demonstrate what commitment means for individuals and groups.

Discuss:

What might it mean for our church to recognize and acknowledge its "minority" status in a foreign culture?

How can we concentrate on creating and/or maintaining communities of faith, regardless of numerical or financial growth?

How can we demonstrate what commitment means for individuals and groups based on the certainty of God's love and compassion?

Conclusion

Consider your own congregation or community in terms of a place where an expression and example of commitment might be helpful. Try to imagine ways to provide such, and then plan to do so.

Passing the Peace

The peace of Christ be with you.
    And also with you.
Amen.

God's Ongoing Plan: A New Covenant

Main Idea
Though Jeremiah declared grave news, that was not his only word. Destruction, plucking up, was to come, but so were building and planting. God's work was not over. God still had a plan that deeply involved both Israel and Judah.

Preparing to Lead
- Read and reflect on chapter 6, "God's Ongoing Plan: A New Covenant."
- Review this plan for the group gathering, and select questions and activities that you will use.
- What other questions, issues, or themes occur to you from your reflection?

Gathering
- Provide simple refreshments as people arrive and name tags if needed.

Opening Worship
Prayer (unison)
O God of hope, continue to assure us of your loving care. When we get despondent, grant that we may see the world as you do with all its possibilities. When a sense of futility and defeat captures us, free us that we may claim with enthusiasm and conviction the opportunities that you offer. You are creating a new world! Help us to participate in your glorious work. In Jesus' name we pray. Amen.

Prayerful, Reflective Reading
- Read Jeremiah 31:31–34 aloud.
- Invite all to reflect for a few minutes in silence.

- After reflection time, invite all to listen for a word or phrase as the passage is read again and to reflect on that word or phrase in silence.
- Read the passage a third time, asking all to offer a silent prayer following the reading.
- Invite volunteers to share the word or phrase that spoke most deeply to them.

Prayer

Loving God, hear our prayers today as we seek to follow you more faithfully:

(*spoken prayers may be offered*)

Hear us now as we pray together, saying, Our Father . . .

Conversation

- Introduce chapter 6, "God's Ongoing Plan: A New Covenant." Share observations, reflections, and insights.
- Review the Introduction (pp. 39–40). Share these key points:
  a. Chapters 30–31 of Jeremiah have been named the "Book of Consolation."
  b. The Northern Kingdom has been destroyed in punishment and scattered in exile. But the people will be redeemed and brought back to their homeland (18–22; 30:10–11).
  c. Jeremiah envisions that God intends a "new covenant."
  Ask the participants to read Exodus 20:1–18. As soon as they have finished reading, ask for a volunteer. Do not yet tell why. Instruct the participants to close their Bibles. Ask the volunteer to quote the passage, word for word. If this volunteer gives up, ask if others want to try.
  When any who wish have tried, invite the participants to again open their Bibles to the same passage. Looking at the commandments one at a time, discuss whether the participants believe that they would or would not know to obey each specific commandment if they were not reading it or had never read it. How do they know?
  Discuss:

  When God promised to put a new covenant in the hearts of the people, what do you think that meant to them?

- Review "A Basic Theme: God's Restoration of Hope" (pp. 40–41). Share these key points:
  a. God intends to restore Israel. God will exercise compassion so that there may be restoration.
  b. God's instrument of reclamation will be a new covenant that God will establish with Israel-Judah. The "old covenant" was good and should have been sufficient, but the people—not God—broke it and went away from God (31:32).
  c. God would write the new law on their hearts, not on stone tablets. The people then would be capable of knowing God (31:33).

Read aloud the following verses, and name what had happened to the hearts of God's people since the time of Moses: Jeremiah 7:22–26; 9:12–13; 9:25–26; and 11:6–8.

Invite the participants to name some of the ways that Judah's tumultuous situation in Jeremiah's time seems similar to what we experience now.

- Review "The Life of Faith: Accepting God's Gift of Hope" (pp. 42–43). Share these key points:
  a. To accept God's gracious gift at least two things are immediately necessary: 1) belief that there is a God and 2) the recognition of how seriously one has disappointed (sinned against) God.
  b. It is difficult to believe that God can and will just forgive our trespasses because we have long been taught that we have to earn God's love and favor by being "good."
  c. We need one another to remind us that God has already forgiven us and offered us the wonderful gift of hope.

Genuine hoping is different from merely wishing. Hope triggers expectation, and expectation produces action. Discuss:

What kind of expectations and actions does trusting that God's work of restoration is ongoing produce?

How might you and your church contribute to God's work?

Discuss:

What are some concrete ways of helping others (as well as yourself) really accept God's forgiveness and put aside old fears and self-criticism?

- Review "The Church: A Message of Restorative Hope" (pp. 43–44). Share these key points:
  a. The task of the church now is to keep urging people to hope and work toward that new world God intends.
  b. We can agitate for change in governmental policy. We can support programs that are aimed at assisting the poor: food pantries, lunch programs, housing repairs, aids for the homeless, health clinics, foster care for needful children, programs of care for the aging, and so on and on.
  Reflect on Parker's hymn (p. 44), and sketch out other ways to "live into hope." Consider some practical steps you and your congregation might take to move forward more intentionally toward hope.

Conclusion

Invite the group to "adopt" a project dealing with refugees. Most denominations have programs that minister to refugees, migrant workers, persons in prison, or others who are in "exile" from the community.

On a large sheet of paper, list possible ways to serve exiles. The easiest would be to make a cash gift. But there may be opportunities near your community. Migrant workers or persons coming from another country to work in your area would be a possibility for a service project. Local social service agencies would be a reliable source of information about how to be most helpful to these persons.

Steps in the process might include:

1. Gather more information. A team from the group could meet with local persons to get more information or a team could do research on the Web about refugee ministries supported by your denomination.
2. Decide what the group will do.

3. Raise money, gather supplies, or whatever next steps you need to take.
4. If your response is some kind of "hands-on" project, agree on a date and time, plan for transportation, and so on.
5. Plan for time after the project to discuss perceptions, learnings, and feelings.

Passing the Peace
The peace of Christ be with you.
   And also with you.
Amen.

Glossary*

covenant. The binding or establishing of a bond between two parties.

exile. The period of the Jews' captivity in ancient Babylon (587–538 BCE). Also known as the Babylonian captivity.

heart. Biblically, the center of the human person from which emotions and values arise. God knows the heart (1 Samuel 16:7).

new covenant. The anticipated action of God in establishing a relationship of the heart with people, seen in Christianity as fulfilled in Jesus Christ.

prophecy. Speaking on behalf of God to communicate God's will. It is also used for the prediction or declaration of what will come to pass in the future.

prophet. One who speaks on behalf of God to God's people, most prominently the Hebrew prophets whose writings are found in the Old Testament.

---

* The definitions here relate to ways these terms are used in this study. Further explorations can be made in other resources, such as Donald K. McKim, *The Westminster Dictionary of Theological Terms*, 2nd ed. (Louisville, KY: Westminster John Knox Press, 2014).

Want to Know More?

Brueggemann, Walter. *A Commentary on Jeremiah*. Grand Rapids: Wm. B. Eerdmans Publishing Co., 1998.

Clements R. E. *Jeremiah*. Interpretation. A Bible Commentary for Teaching and Preaching. Louisville, KY: Westminster John Knox Press, 1988.

Heschel, Abraham J. *The Prophets*. New York: Harper & Row, 1962 (particularly chs. 12–14 in the one-volume edition and chs. 1–5, part 2, of the two-volume edition)

Laha, Robert. *Jeremiah*. Interpretation Bible Studies. Louisville, KY: Westminster John Knox Press, 2008.

O'Connor, Kathleen M. *Jeremiah: Pain and Promise*. Minneapolis: Fortress Press, 2011.

CPSIA information can be obtained
at www.ICGtesting.com
Printed in the USA
FFHW011934170819
54372085-60072FF